This is Me

Brittany Evans

BookLeaf Publishing

India | USA | UK

Presentation by *BookLeaf Publishing*

Web: www.bookleafpub.com

E-mail: info@bookleafpub.com

ISBN: 9789360942472

First edition 2024

*For my hubby who always goes with my crazy
ideas and sees me with rose-colored glasses*

*For my kiddos who have brought so much joy
and love into my life*

For my students who never cease to amaze me

For my besties who are always there for me

*For my kindred spirit who gets so mad at me,
but loves me, and is always by my side*

*and to God who gave me all of these blessings
and so much more*

This is Me

Who did God create me to be?

 He has made me...

    a daughter and granddaughter
    a wife (17 years and counting)
    a mother of 3
    a friend
    a kindred spirit
    a teacher
    a pastor's wife

    a woman who has made many mistakes but is not forsaken
    a woman who was lost but now is found
    a woman who tries to keep it together and then has to hand it over to God
    a woman who struggles with her thoughts at times
    a woman who says it like it is
    a woman who doesn't say something unless she means it
    a woman who is an overcomer

a woman who has to teach big words at times, but outside of school is not super refined with an eloquent vocabulary

a woman who owns all of the Fast and Furious movies

a woman who would love to be ballroom dancer or a drag racer

a woman who loves of Jesus, coffee, cheesecake, the ocean, Selena, Patrick Swayze, and Coke Zero

a woman who is simple yet complicated.

I am certain that as I continue to walk through this adventurous life, I will continue to add to and modify this list.

And whether life is going good, bad, ugly, and/or a little of all three, God will be there to help me get through it. He knows my shortcomings and my strengths...afterall, He did create me.

Tidal Waves

My life is like an ocean
full of defining and uncontrollable moments
it can be exciting yet sometimes is unpredictable
as I start to move from the shoreline each day
until I reach where the sun touches the water
I encounter serenity and peace full of laughter,
love, kindness, and joy
and then when I least expect it
monstrous waves of sadness, disparity, anger,
and broken trust
come crashing down upon me and my loved
ones
the current can get to be so strong that it tries to
pull me so far under where is hard to catch air
hard to keep swimming
hard to keep fighting
hard to breathe...
but then when all feels hopeless and lost
there's a glimmer of HOPE that appears
and when I reach for it and grasp it
it brings me back to the surface
to keep fighting
to keep swimming
to keep breathing
thank you, Jesus.

When we first met...

When we first met...

I didn't want to know you.

I had no desire to talk to you.

I remember walking through the garage, and my dad was forcing me to say hello because you were the new lead singer and guitar player of his band.

I said my hello, rolled my eyes, and walked away.

I was still in highschool.

I wanted to get a job, save up, go to college, and get out.

I felt so sad, angry, and disappointed on the inside.

I was going through a lot with my family.

I coped in the wrong ways, and felt broken.

I wasn't expecting anything great to come along.

I never had any desire to ever get married let alone have children.

I had no clue what it meant to be in a healthy relationship.

I confided in very few people.

I doubted that you actually cared.

I was unaware that I was going to fall in love with a rockin' blues player, which was something that I told myself I was never going to do.

After some time...
I realized that you did really love me, and I loved you back.
I believed in us as a couple.
I could picture us married, children, and building a life together.
I knew that we would be together for a long time.
I learned how to love myself better and who Jesus was.
We got pregnant.
We got married.
We had a family.
We were accountable to each other.
We were happy.

But then...
it got hard.
It wasn't fun anymore.
It was like we were on different sides of the world.
It spiraled out of control.
It felt as if there was no love or kindness left.

Until...
  God.
  God spoke to you.
  God saved us.
  God redirected us, and we listened.
  God brought us back to each other.

And then...
  we beat the odds.
  We came back as one not two.
  We added to our family.
  We were starting to listen to what God was
wanting for us individually and as a couple.
  We were Curt and Britt again.

Now...
  we love more than before.
  We still annoy one another just like before.
  We give more grace and forgiveness than
before.
  We show more kindness and intentionality
than before.
  We are trying our best to raise our kids in a
God loving home more than before.

I can't wait...
  to see who our amazing children turn out to be.
  To watch how the Lord uses you, me, us, and
our family to expand His kingdom.

To go on all the epic adventures and trips that we have not yet taken.

To reach our 50th wedding anniversary and be able to tell so many unbelievable stories.

To retire oceanside with you.

I love you Curtis, my forever blues man.

My Cup of Jo

A good cup of coffee
is strong and bold
underestimated
needed
loved by many
and is essential to my everyday existence.

Come to think about it… my husband is like a
good cup of coffee.

He is strong and bold
underestimated
needed
and loved by many
and is essential to my everyday existence.

A good cup of coffee
isn't bitter or have an acidic aftertaste
and it most definitely is a BLESSING from God
and is essential to my everyday existence.

My husband is like a good cup of coffee
he isn't bitter and doesn't have an acidic
aftertaste
he is most definitely a blessing from God,

and He is essential to my everyday existence.

A good cup of coffee usually has a flavor that's poppin
and my husband is like the whipped cream that I use for my topping. (Yeah...I went there. No worries, I'll leave it PG.)

I'm so grateful that my husband is part of my everyday existence.

Yahtzee!

This is me and my husband.

I'm sure you have heard the expression "opposites attract." Well, from my experience, it can be really hard to make the "opposites attract" relationship work. It can be that way for many reasons. Because of all the differences, it can be hard to find excitement and passion for each other and for the things the other person loves to do after so long. It takes time and effort. I also know it can be so electrifying at first because there's so much love and compassion, but then life makes it challenging and what brought you together may not seem like enough. Once again, it takes time and effort. And then there's the part of the relationship where it starts to go through battle after battle because the enemy wants to see it fail, but the people try to resist, and they overcome. Not that they didn't fail along the way, but they persevere and withstand the storms together. Each person in a relationship has a choice…they have the choice to stick it out, the choice to stand strong and to lean on each other and God, or the choice to end it. My husband and I made the choice to keep fighting for us and our family.

This is me and my husband.

We've been together for almost 20 years, and when I think about how my grandparents have been together for almost 60 years, I think to myself…hmm…that's a really long time. To be fair, I'm sure that my hubby thinks that way about me sometimes. He He. Even as I write this he is being obnoxiously annoying and playful all at the same time in the kitchen, which to be fair I like, but he doesn't need to know that. I wouldn't want to annoy anyone else or be annoyed by anyone else.

This is me and my husband.

When I think about where we have been, what Jesus has done for us, what we have been through, and how EXTREMELY different we are as people I know that the next however many years we have together will be nothing short of unexpected awesomeness, and our love will continue to grow. I know this because I love you more now than ever before.

This is me and my husband.

There was a time where once again we were
going in completely different directions when
we were supposed to be heading in the same
one. I never imagined that we would be where
we are right now, together. But God obviously
has some awesome plans for us as a couple.

This is me and my husband.

He likes fishing, I don't.
He likes hunting, I won't.
He likes all kinds of music including folk, that's
a no.
He likes strong black coffee, I need a solid
cream to coffee ratio.
He likes the colors blue and red, and mine are
coral, purple, and teal.
He likes to leave the cereal on the counter
without closing the seal!
He likes to camp, I'd prefer to not.
He can rock the guitar, I can't play, but I do think
it's hot. (wink wink)
He plays games to play, I play to win.
We play YAHTZEE quite often, but I'm the one
usually at the end with a grin.
If you watch us as we play, one would plainly
see
that we are very different even in our strategies.

This is me and my husband.

Curtis, this is my message for you...

I love you with all of my heart, and I know that
you just love my dutch ovens when we're in bed
and I decide to fart.
Even though you get cold, and I get hot
you like your steak rare, and I absolutely do
NOT
you are cheesy, I like to rhyme
I hope that I can play YAHTZEE with you for a
really long time.

Leah Alene

Who is my Leah Alene?

She is a little girl that can make anyone around her smile or laugh with her lighthearted and silly wit.

She is a little girl that can love so big and tenaciously that when she wraps her arms around your neck you have to tell her to let go or not to squeeze so tight.

She is a little girl that is so beautiful with her golden locks, pale blue eyes, and the cutest little freckles on her cheeks.

She is a little girl who can be amazingly sweet and savage at the same time.

She is a little girl with an imagination as big as the world who pretends to fight bad guys, cooks for her babies, and teaches her students all the things.

She is a little girl who sings with joy and repetition to all of her favorite songs until they become your favorite songs as well.

She is a little girl who dances with all that she can give and acts like she owns the floor.

She is a little girl whose smile lights up the room and who reminds me to smile just a little more.

She is a little girl who we prayed for and who God entrusted us with.

She is a little girl who brings my husband and I great happiness, as well as, to anyone who is around her.

She is a little girl that touches my soul and inspires me everyday to be a better person…a better mom.

She is a little girl that I promise to love with all of my heart, soul, and being.

She is a little girl who is remarkable and extraordinary and who will shine her light anywhere she goes.

That is my Leah Alene.

Around the World with the Jack-Man

Ladies first
Swoosh!
Bam what!
All net.
Did you see that?
You want some of this?
Woot woot!
Ahh...the sun was in my eyes.
Now, it's your turn.
Nice.
Oops.
Back to me.
This corner!
Ugh.
It's your go Jack-Man.
Let's see what you got.
Very nice.
Watch your form, kid.
Let me show you.
Say what?
That's how you do it!
Swish.
Ugh.
Back to the corner.

Next time.
It's your shot Jack-Man.
There you go.
That's what I'm talking about.
Get it boy.
It looks good.
Nope.
Next time.
Sorry baby, I'm going to finish it.
There's one.
There's two.
And there's three.
Momma wins again.
Love you.

There will come a day when my Jack-Man will
out b-ball me
and that will be super awesome to see
but for now
I'll just enjoy teaching him how to talk a little
smack, shoot the ball, do a crossover, and play
some D-E.

You, my Jack-Man, are a handsome, one of a
kind guy
who is so fly
with so many skills and beautiful blue eyes
who is meant for extreme greatness, which is no
surprise

so shoot for the stars, Jackson Curtis
and just remember that your dad, myself, and
God will always be by your side.

Lillyan Grace

Words cannot explain how proud of you I am.

It seems as if only yesterday we were bringing you home with those cute chunky cheeks and big beautiful brown eyes.

It seems as if only yesterday when I would rock you and think about how scared I was to be a mother but so beyond thankful that God let me have the chance.

It seems as if only yesterday you were learning to walk, talk, and do all the things. Oh how you were ornery and fiesty… and oh how some things don't change.

It seems as if only yesterday you were just starting Kindergarten in those cute little black shoes and the hot pink backpack.

Your father and I really did not know what we were doing..let us be real about that. And, there may have been that time I dropped on you accident in the car seat… or threw a piece of corn at you, and it got stuck on your jugular…and I could not stop laughing… or the fact that we moved quite a bit, and not to mention your dad and I did at one point did not have a relationship with Jesus or each other, wait...you also had a couple of car accidents you were in (one being a semi), plus all the extra trauma that you went through...these are just to name a few.

You have shown that you are RESILIENT, STRONG, TENACIOUS, COURAGEOUS, and AMAZING. Do not ever forget that your story is going to help so many, and God will use it for His glory. Just remember that through your tough times, good times, mistakes, failures, and successes, I will always love you, my Lillyan Grace.

Don't Mess with a Mother

How dare you?
   Disgusting
   Nauseating
   Revolting
That's you...you know who you are. Those are
some of the adjectives I could use to describe
you...the person who hurt my baby.

You thought it was okay to take what didn't
belong to you?
  How dare you?

You thought it was okay to take joy that wasn't
yours?
  How dare you?

You thought it was okay to create unwanted
anxiety and fear that can rise up at any moment?
  How dare you?

You thought you could get away with it?
  How dare you?

You thought there wouldn't be any
consequences?

How dare you?

You thought you could mess with the love of a
mother?
    YOU were wrong.

What you didn't think about was that...

God is bigger than this.
God is a just God.
God is a healer.
God hears my prayers.
And God made me a mother who fiercely loves
her children and who will do whatever it takes to
do whatever necessary to get the job done.

How dare you think you won?

Promises

To my babies:

Growing up I never had the desire or passion to be a mother…
that was until I saw the most beautiful brown eyes staring up at me.
It was a feeling that I will never forget. Up until that point in my life, I had never felt that way before. The feelings of complete and utter terror, because I was now responsible for a life other than my own, and love that was so rich it was overwhelming. It was a love that was unconditional and pure. It was one of the most joyful moments of my life. I am so blessed because I got to have this moment not only once, but three times, except for the other two times…they were blue eyes.

Lillyan Grace, Jackson Curtis, and Leah Alene you are three of the most precious gifts that God has ever given me so these promises are for you.

I promise you... that every second of every day you are loved and cared for.
I promise you... that when you feel like giving up, I will be there for you even when you don't want me to be.

I promise you... that when you make a mistake, I will love you.

I promise you... that when you are successful, whether in school, sports, video games (yeah Jack I am referring to you there), life, etc., I will share that excitement with you.

I promise you... that I will fight for you, and I will have your back. (Now, if you're in the wrong, I will help you with owning that.)

I promise you... that when we play games you will have to win on your own accord because I will not let you win. (Leahgirl…you're already beating me at the UNO and Candyland so I have no doubt you will keep showing me what's up.)

I promise you... that I will be an awesome grandmother to your children someday.

I promise you... that even when you are grown I will be present in your life. Sorry about yah...that's just how it works.

I promise you... that we have many more family vacations and "adventures" to embark on.

I promise you... that I might tell you to tuck and roll.

I promise you... that your dad and I might gross you out a time or two.

I promise you... that your dad and I's marriage is not perfect, but we love each other very much.

I promise you...that I will always try to be the best mother I can be for you; however, I also promise you that I will fail, and I have already multiple times, but God is so gracious and is always teaching me.

I promise you...that you can always count on me to give you a hug when you need it, and even when you say you don't. (Right, Toots?)

I promise you... that when you feel all the feels, I feel all the feels.

I promise you... that when you don't know what to do with all those feels, I am here to help you navigate them.

I promise you... that I won't always have the answers, but I will surely try to come up with something good.

I promise you... that God knew you before you were born.

I promise you... that God created you with a purpose.

I promise you... that God hand-picked your dad and I to be your parents, and there's not a day that goes by that we would want it any other way.

I love you.

Love,
Mom

Where's mom?

Oh bathroom, how I love you so!
My soul longs for the time we spend with one another
even when I don't actually have to go.

I get so excited to come home from school,
that the first thing I do is take off my shoes,
put my stuff away, change my clothes,
and head to the loo.

You are such a good friend
who listens, supports, and doesn't disagree.
Our relationship has no bounds or ends
and everyone around us can plainly see.

You know me, my heart, my mind, and my desires
and every time I step foot within your threshold
whether I feel put together or like being a crier,
you stretch out your hand, and pull me right into
an environment that is in my control.

As I close my eyes and listen to the solitary bliss
of my brain being shut off from ideas,
expectations, and the world,

I rather enjoy the still quietness,
and I think to myself how did I ever become
such a lucky girl.

Thank you bathroom for all the rinsing, flushing,
scrubbing, and washing my troubles away
and helping me to rejuvenate myself
so that I can be on my merry way
and confidently grab that toilet paper on the
shelf
Because the footsteps will start to come and the
hubby and kids will start to knock
and it's not fair to them if I'm not my best self.

Even if it only lasts for 30 seconds, a minute,
maybe two or three,
I will always cherish the moments we have
together
because you are my own personal hideout where
I can go to just breathe
and you, my bathroom, I feel as if there are no
storms we cannot weather.

Before the Coffee...

Have you ever felt like your name was said a
MILLION times in one day?

Sometimes, it feels like my name is said a
MILLION times before I even finish my coffee.

(I take my first big sip of coffee before my
students enter the room.)

7:10 Good morning Mrs. Evans.
7:11 Hi Mrs. Evans.
7:12 Hey, Mrs. Evans, guess what?
7:12 Good morning, Mrs. Evans, look at this!
7:14 Mrs. Evans, where do you want the
homework?
7:15 Mrs. Evans, can I get the stool?
7:17 Mrs. Evans, can I get the other one?

(I take another sip.)

7:19 Mrs. Evans, can I use the bathroom?
7:20 Hey, Mrs. Evans.
7:21 Morning, Mrs. Evans.
7:23 Mrs. Evans, my chromebook isn't working.
7:24 Hey, Mrs. Evans, what's for lunch?

7:25 Mrs. Evans, do we have Art today?
7:27 Do you want me to turn on the morning show, Mrs. Evans?
7:29 Mrs. Evans, is it supposed to be cold today? I didn't bring a coat?
7:30 Is it supposed to rain, Mrs. Evans? I want to go out for recess.
7:31 Do you want me to turn it up more, Mrs. Evans?

(I take another long sip of coffee.)

7:40 What was lunch A again, Mrs. Evans?
7:45 What activity are we going to do again for morning meeting, Mrs. Evans?

(Another long sip...)

7:47 Mrs. Evans, he won't stop touching my desk.
7:50 Mrs. Evans, can I start the silent ball?
7:57 Mrs. Evans, can we play another round?

(Another long sip...)

8:00 Mrs. Evans, is this the right paper?
8:05 Mrs. Evans, I know the answer!

(Sip...)

8:10 Mrs. Evans, can I read the next paragraph?

(Sip, sip, sip)

8:22 Mrs. Evans, aren't we supposed to line up
now for Art?

(Ahh...followed by another sip and a yes)

How many times is my name said in a day?
Well...it's obviously too many to count, list, or
say.

The amount that takes place before I can even
drink all of my coffee sometimes makes me
want to overindulge with some melt in your
mouth chocolate and crunchy toffee.

But even though my students say my name
for what feels like a million or bazillion times a
day,
I love them, anyhow and anyway.
Yes, my students do have a lot to say,
and yes it makes me feel a little cray cray.

But regardless, I love them so,
even if I can't get through my cup of Jo.

Definitely NOT Ordinary

To all of my past, present, and even future
students...

You know who I find to be
EXTRAORDINARY?
You!
All of you!
I believe that every single one of you are
EXTRAORDINARY
even if you don't feel like you are.

Each one of you contains the "X" factor.
You may not even know what it is yet,
but the point is that you have it,
and I believe you have it.

According to Webster's, EXTRAORDINARY is
defined as being REMARKABLE,
EXCEPTIONAL, SPECIAL, UNUSUAL,
MARVELOUS, NOTEWORTHY, UNIQUE,
AND RARE.
I believe this to be true about all of you.

You were all born for goodness,

and my hope for you is that one day you will
believe it and use it to do great things to help
others.

I believe EXTRAORDINARY is a feeling also.
And when I'm teaching you, it makes me feel
EXTRAORDINARY because I get to be a part
of your lives.
I get to see your successes and help you through
your struggles.

EXTRAORDINARY is something special that
lies within each and everyone of you
BUT
It's up to you to let it shine!

Once a YJ, Always a YJ

This is a shout out to all the YJs.

Stand up (Clap clap)
Be proud (Clap clap)
Say your name (Clap clap)
Out loud (Clap clap)
We are the YJs! (Repeat)

Anyone who has ever stepped foot into the YJ
gym knows that chant by heart,
so for all of the current, past, and future YJs,
let's break it down from the start.

Stand up:
   Listen to me when I say to stand up for what is
right
   and to put up a fight
   and not to lose sight
   to give all your might
   to help, encourage, and guide those who may
feel like there's no more light.

Be proud:
   As each of you get older and try to figure out
who you are,

and try to remember this...
Be a person who is honest
and who works hard for what you want in life
and what you desire
    don't get lazy or act too tired
    or create muck and mire
    or be an untrusted liar
    but instead...
    be proud of what you've done and inspire.

Say your name:
    You might be wondering really…Mrs. Evans,
why is this necessary?
    My answer is simple and honestly could be
quite legendary.
    There's no real good reason to be ashamed to
say your name
    unless you've done something wrong
    in which you feel shame
    if that's the case, just apologize and move on
    so don't live in vain
    or regrets on the brain.

We are the YJs:
    This signifies a family...
    maybe a little dysfunctional with a little
insanity
    but nonetheless in all actuality
    a family helps maintain your center of gravity.

So stand up, be proud, say your name, out loud,
because you are forever a YJ, and that won't
ever go away.

From Me to You

A better you? A better me
if only we could open our eyes to see
that spreading God's love is what we need to to
do
to be a better me...to be a better you...
To be a better US

The world is full of darkness and despair
it's our job to do our best, love one another, and
shine His light
so things can start to repair

All the negatives
the beatdowns
the unkind words
just do unto others as you'd want done unto you
that's the only way anyone will really be heard
and that's the truth

So in order to be a better you, a better me, a
better US...

Just be KIND humans
who care about doing right and who cares about
others

and who aren't blind to how our differences can
be used for good

We don't have to hate, berate, or stand in the way
we can stand together to make the world better
by...

SMILING more
SAYING "Hi" more
DANCING more
GIVING grace more
BEING a peacemaker more
HAVING a relationship with JESUS more

Open your beautiful eyes and see that all of
these things can make a better you, a better me,
a better US.

I Am Mrs. Evans

*To every crew

I am Mrs. Evans, and I always have the best
crews.
I wonder if they know how much I love and care
about each and every one of them.
I hear my crew when they get frustrated, excited,
sad, angry, anxious, and happy.
I see my crew work hard and get stuff done.
I would like to see my crew show more kindness
towards one another even when frustrated.
I want you all to be successful in your own way.
I am Mrs. Evans, and I always have the best
crew.

I pretend that I live by the ocean, and that I have
class on the warm sand, but since I don't actually
live by the ocean, being here with you all in this
classroom is the next best thing.
I feel like I was born to be a teacher, and I know
I was meant to be YOUR teacher.
I touch success when you feel successful.
I worry about each of you.
I cry thinking about what some of you go
through on a day to day basis.

I am Mrs. Evans, and I always have the best crew.

I understand some days are harder than others and mistakes happen.
I say "I believe in you," "I love you all," and "We got this" everyday because it's true.
I dream that my crew keeps moving on even when it gets tough.
I try to create fun and enjoyment even when the material may not be that exciting.
I hope that you will never forget that they are all special to me.

I am Mrs. Evans, and I always have the BEST crew.

Grams

Thank you for always loving me
for all the Christmas joy, swags, lights, and
magical trees
for being one of the only places where I felt
truly safe and free
thank you for always unconditionally loving me

Thank you for the beautiful memories of
Christmas enchantment, sparkle, and magic
and for the delicious and delightful food that you
worked so hard to prepare through and through
and even though it never took long to
devour...one thing is for certain, it was the best
and that's the truth
but none of it would have even mattered if it
wasn't with you

Thank you for listening to me when no one else
would
Thank you for caring for me when no one else
could
Thank you for putting me in my place when I
needed to be as well as reminding me what I was
capable of when someone else should have

Thank you for showing me that even when life
around me seemed so bad, I could choose to be
good

Thank you for teaching me to stand tall, to have
hope, and to be optimistic so that the craziness
of life can be withstood

I love you so very much, and I know God used
you in a mighty way and to keep me in His
clutch
because without you I'm not sure if I would have
survived or felt the embrace of an earthly hand
or a gentle touch

So thank you grams ...
for being my safe haven
for being so inspiring
and once again thank you for always loving me
UNCONDITIONALLY

Camp Memories

I remember when I went to church camp every
summer.
It holds a very dear place in my heart and some
of the best and most favorite memories as a kid.
When the week was over, I always thought to
myself, "Why did it have to end so soon?"

I remember when I went to church camp every
summer with my grandparents. I will never
forget all of the laughing, swimming, carpet
balling, crafting, church attending, singing, sheet
volleyballing, hiking, capture the flagging, horse
riding, and canteening. When the week was
over, I always thought to myself, "Why did it
have to end so soon?"

I remember when I went to church camp every
summer with my grandparents, cousin Sarah,
and my uncle's family. Oh, the amount of times
we would try to shove each other under the
water in the pool, watch my uncle and grandpa
do epic dives off the diving board, race to the
horse sign-up sheet every day after lunch to get
the best horse, watch gramps champ it up at the
horseshoe competition, watch grandma sing

beautiful hymns, and take extra long walks to the sign and back that seemed to last forever at the time but now are precious memories to think about. When the week was over, I always thought to myself, "Why did it have to end so soon?"

I remember when I went to church camp every summer, and as I got older it didn't seem as cool, and the excitement started to dwindle...dwindle until we turned onto the rocky path by the sign that read "Camp Manitoumi." It wasn't long before I saw the horse stables on the left, the ball fields and church building on the right, and as we went a little further you would see the brick cabins, and still further there was the pool and food hall. The excitement that wasn't present when I was first picked up started to flood back instantly. As soon as we got our suitcases out of the car and headed into the cabin, my cousin and I would argue over which thin mattressed bunk bed we wanted. My cousin and I would even have a system in how we would put our clothes, bedding, toiletries, and fan. This was exciting to us. This was really the only time Sarah and I would get to hang out so we always made the most of it. I was younger so I could easily annoy her, which was also fun, but we clicked, and it was so nice to have someone to talk to. We rode

so many horses on so many trails together. I
learned how to trot, canter, and gallop from her.
Even though I had fallen off multiple times, was
kicked, stomped on, and even bit, I loved every
second with the horses and with Sarah. We may
have gotten into trouble a time or two by our
grandparents, but for the moment, I just
remember being happy. When the week was
over, I always asked myself, "Why did it have to
end so soon?"

I remember when I went to church camp every
summer with my grandparents. I am so grateful
to them that year after year they would pick me
up from my dad's house and drive us, to what
felt like a million miles away when in reality it
was a few towns over. I didn't know at the time
that this amazing place would be forever etched
in my heart and mind. Grandpa, do you
remember walking to the church with the family,
and you stepped on a "frog." Ha Ha. I will never
forget grandma and Sarah looking around
frantically for it, and that frog never to be found.
Grandma, do you remember making Sarah and I
sing with you often at church, and we acted like
we didn't want to? Surely, you know it did bring
a little bit of joy, and as adults, we thank you for
spending that time with us. I thank you both for
these moments and so many more. I thank you

for all the time, energy, and love you gave to me during that week. It filled me up and gave me such joy. And when that week was over, I remember thinking to myself every time, "Why do we have to leave so soon?"

First Lady

A couple years ago as I walked into church, one of the kindest and sweetest women came over to me, hugged me, and joyfully said, "It's so good to see our First Lady."

Excuse me.

I just smiled and hugged her back. At this time, my husband was a campus pastor and led worship, but I didn't feel like I had a role. I was definitely intimidated by those words, and it was so weird how two words brought such mixed emotions and made me feel so inadequate. It sounded so important, and I was struggling to feel that way. To be honest, I didn't like the phrase "First Lady" at all, but I went with it because I loved her. She continued to call me that every time she saw me.

It wasn't until my husband became the lead pastor of an amazing church in South Carolina that I started to truly feel like I had that role of a "First Lady." It still freaks me out at times. These people are so supportive, I get asked questions and my opinion is valued, and I am

watched a little more. It makes me giggle to
think that God put me in this role, but I know
that He knows way more than me and has plans
for me that I don't even know about.

You see, I do not like to fail at things, and when
I come into something new, I like to be prepared.
If I do fail at something or think that I will not
do well, I try to do a little research so I can
prevent said things from happening. That's
exactly what I did. According to the internet and
my own understanding, this is what a "First
Lady" should be like...

a director of social affairs
a liason
a symbol of strength
a lover of our country
a policy advocate
a reformer
a friend to the people
a confidante to the lead man
a hostess
an influencer
an advocate for rights
a trendsetter
and someone who can be criticized for doing
too much or too little

I don't know about you, but there is no way I can measure up to that list. I'm not one that has many insecurities, but I know I am not perfect, and at some point, I'm sure I'll get something wrong. When it's just the Lord and I, I even tend to question him.

I question whether I'm cut out to lead groups or events.
I question whether or not I can give sound advice because I don't know everything there is to know in the Bible, and what if someone comes to me, and I don't know the proper answer.
I question if I can do this because sometimes the Lord needs me to stay quiet, and I have a hard time doing this.
I question if I have enough etiquette.
I question if I can do this because I don't have the same outgoing, extroverted, people person loving attitude as my husband.
I question a lot of things.

And then as always, I am reminded by God that I am made in His image, and I can do these things, and that I am enough. I know that I can't please everyone, just ask my husband, but I promise to do my ultimate best, and when there are mistakes, I will own them. I also promise to

love this church, its people, community, and to
be in prayer. Being the "First Lady" of Camden
Naz is a role that I was meant to have, and it is
an honor.

Mis Amigas

Always
can count on them
to be encouraging
truthful, loyal and supportive
love them

Kimberly—
Close friend
Intelligent
Loved by many children
Gave her heart to her family
Miss Kim

Krista—
Homegirl
Approachable
Big-hearted and savage
Beautiful both inside and out
Rosa

Mary-
Best friend
Dependable
Fabulous and star-like
Knowledgeable and generous

Beauty

Emily—
K.S.
Hilarious
Resilient and thoughtful
Diligent and empathetic
H.B.

Kindred Spirit

My K.S. is...
    beautiful and gracious of her time
    selfless, compassionate, and who I can get
mad at me easily
    amazing and sooo funny with her crazy facial
expressions
    and is worth so much more than what she
believes.

My K.S. has...
    a contagious spirit
    a fresh energy and a wonderful voice that she
says is only used for the Lord
    the best birthday ever, "because it's not too hot,
not too cold, and all you
    need is a light jacket"
    and has so much impact on those around her
that she doesn't even see.

My K.S. needs to...
    know there is extreme greatness meant for her
    realize that her future is so very bright
    see the beauty in herself that she sees in others
    and needs to realize that she is so much
stronger than what she believes.

My K.S. brings...
    my heart joy
    me conversations that others may not
understand
    laughter that is needed and may have made me
pee my pants
    and brings me back down when I'm feeling
fierce.

My K.S. is...
    my bestie for the restie
    someone who I can tell anything to and who
will give me honest responses
    a person who God put in my life for a reason
    and is one of my favorite people in the entire
world.